Saints & Cannibals

Christine Hamm

Plain View Press
P. O. 42255
Austin, TX 78704

plainviewpress.net
sb@plainviewpress.net
512-441-2452

Copyright Christine Hamm 2010. All rights reserved under International and Pan-American Copyright Conventions. No part of this book may be reproduced or distributed in any form or by any means, or stored in a data base or retrieval system, without written permission from the author. All rights, including electronic, are reserved by the author and her publisher.

ISBN: 978-1-935514-40-4
Library of Congress Number: 2010920351

Cover art by Christine Hamm
Cover design by Susan Bright

Acknowledgments

Some of these poems have appeared in the following works and journals: "The Transparent Dinner", "Memoir of an Unrepentant Thief", "The Weight of the World", "Territory", "Truth or Dare" and "Joy School" in *The Transparent Dinner* (book by Christine Hamm, published by Mayapple Press); "The Transparent Dinner", "Aspirin," and "Stable" in *The Animal Husband* (chapbook by Christine Hamm, published by Dancing Girl Press); "Territory" in *The Salt Daughter* (chapbook by Christine Hamm, published by Little Poem Press);"Children Having Trouble with Meat", "How the Witch Got Started" and "Qualities of Sugar" in *Children Having Trouble with Meat* (chapbook by Christine Hamm, published by MiPoesias); "How the Witch Got Started" in *The Madhatter's Review*; "The Grass Eater" in *Pebble Lake Review*; "Joy School" in *Absinthe Literary Review*; "Joy School" in *The Adirondack Review*; "Truth or Dare" in *VLQ*; "Begin at the Mouth" in *MiPoesias*; "Memoir of an Unrepentant Thief" in *The Goodnight Show*; "March 11th " in *Blue Fifth Review*; "Stable" in *Spire Magazine*; "Modern Maid" in *Nth Position*; "Aspirin" in *The Misfit Library*; "Territory" in *Kitchen Sink*; "How to Make a Person" and "Definition of a Tree" in *Identity Theory*.

To Sylvia

Contents: *Saints & Cannibals*

Saints

Up From the Root Cellar	9
Caldwell, Idaho, 1941	10
Enid Has a Visitor	11
Stable	12
Sophomore	13
Signs You Are Ovulating	14
In This Dream, the Sky Signifies Memory	16
Fertility Rites For a Daughter	17
How To Make a Person (Tail and Background Optional)	18
Frankenstein's Bride	20
Conception	21
Your Birth	22
Begin At the Mouth	23
Definition Of a Tree	24
The Weight Of the World	25
Territory	27
The Grass Eater	28
The Painted Wooden Leg	29
Getting It Down	30
The Snow Queen	31
Memoir Of an Unrepentant Thief	32
The Closet	33
In Stitches	34
The Family Practice	35
Tristessa	36
My Friend Flicka	37
Truth Or Dare	38
Muscular Wrist	40
Susan	41
Leap	42
Ecstasy At 3PM	43
Claire On Sunday	44
Starling	46
The Holy Birds Of Queens	47
Activities Of Daily Living	48
Joy School	49
Perpetual Baptism	50

The Saint of Difficult Furniture	51
Modern Maid	52
The Cul-De-Sac Angel	53
Aspirin	54
March 25, 1911	55

Cannibals

Qualities Of Sugar	59
Children Having Trouble With Meat	61
The Cannibals	62
A Tender Age	64
Supplies	66
The Transparent Dinner	67
How the Witch Got Started	68
Gretel Dreams With Her Eyes Open	71
What We Think About the Missing Girl	72
My Favorite Sacrifice	73
You and Your Animal Teeth	74
What Hansel In His Cage Is Forgetting	75
In the Witch's House, Gretel Remembers	77
The Next Season	78
RRH	79
The Wedding Night	80

About the Author	81

Saints

Up From the Root Cellar

The clouds sometimes look like eyes. On the back porch, Ruby washes tomatoes in a bucket, her apron damp from splashes. Her mother falls, sprawls in the furrows, gingham skirt over her knees, stockings dark with a wet rush. The baby, another baby, is coming. The younger children shriek like crows, stuff dirty fingers in their mouths, clatter into the house. Rachel, the youngest, grabs her mother's hand, tells her to get up. Her mother calls for Ruby. Ruby plucks up a tomato, jams it against her teeth, tasting snow and rust. Her mother yells, *Ruby, Ruby*. Ruby shakes out her skirt, goes to the pump to rinse her hands. She remembers the elephant she touched once at a carnival, big as the sky, wrinkled as a map, dark eye fixed ahead.

Caldwell, Idaho, 1941

at the blackboard, Enid envies the other girls
their slick shoes, the ones not held
together with string, every step
a disaster, waiting

she reads in the library during lunch
carries her bruised apple and bread
in a used paper sack   careful not to tear

she imagines the sea from her books
blue silk, unstained, flowing
like the corn flows in the wind,

dark as the blood pouring from
the throat of an upside down pig

when the puddle reaches Enid's toes
she backs and then backs away again
runs and burrows into the hay
deep down at the bottom is a new nest
with blind kittens like pink fists

her father hates it when the cats give
birth in the hay   the afterbirth molders
the straw   the cows won't eat it

too many cats anyway
her father says when he finds her

Enid Has a Visitor

at first she thought she had rammed
herself too hard against
the horse's withers
when they jumped the gate next
to the broken silo or that her worms were
back   it wasn't blood   it was black and thick

sure she was dying   she ran into the corn
no one could see her
    as she lay down the sun passed over
cramps ripped their way up
                                she vomited

she heard a hum like when she spun and
spun until she fell in the gravel road

the hum of cicadas cresting
        the buzz of crickets as they pulsed into
                                  the night

a cat found her like one always did
they lay together in the dirt
Enid's hands clasped over a round stone
        until she heard her father
                calling her in the dark

Stable

polish and horse tears smear my hands
my boots yanked in the tack room
my hair sticks to snaffle bits and
swaying dressage bridles

my pinto waits, his eyes
follow my hands, ears flick bob,
as I fling saddle over stall door

my face thrusts into his neck
I breathe slow, tongue tip on fur

he shifts from hoof to hoof
stomps at a fly

I make a cradle of my hands
and he rests his chin there
velvet, trembling

Sophomore

              second week of October
     insects still
flinging into street lamps

while you study for
    engineering finals
pencil between your teeth
      you reach a palm right here
           on the side of my neck
                as if to steady me

the library closes
       and we wrap hands
            around knees, braids:
            in your twin bed
    knotted ropes

Signs You Are Ovulating

Colors seem brighter.
You start to confuse your elbows
with your chin, your knees.

You find yourself robbing bodegas
during your lunch break.

Nightingales hover inches from your head
when you step outside. The bird shit
is difficult to get out of your hair,
though you try vinegar.

When you come home from a late night
at Bar None, an elephant is waiting
at the subway station to escort you home.

Every night, gods break into your bedroom.
You push away the swan, tie his neck into a knot.
You hide under the bed to get away
from the black bull, who gores
your hello kitty pillow.

Finally, you soak your underwear
in Raid to ward off
the stubborn stream of gold light
that pours in your window
like insistent neon.

In the morning you wake up
to the sound of the possible people
talking softly inside you.
You turn up your radio
to drown out the noise.

As you apply mascara
in the bathroom, your eyes slits,
a crow hops onto your shoulder,
and whispers, *right here, now*.

In This Dream, the Sky Signifies Memory

I'm standing in my blue flannel nightgown
at the window. The tops of the California oaks
shimmer below me in the wind. I'm walking barefoot
down the center of a gravel road — I'm sweating
and my nightgown pinches at the armpits, the neck.

I am getting a baby out of a drawer. The baby
is the color of fog: he is too heavy to carry,
so I leave him by the side of the road. I am spitting
out persimmon seeds into the cup beside the TV.

I am climbing a ladder over a hedge made of old
keyboards and kites. I am waking up; I am not
wanting to wake up. Someone is calling my cat.
My cat purrs and spits into my eye. She has
gathered tigers around me. I put on my pointed
leather slippers and climb on to the back of
the biggest one. We go searching for my baby.
The sky is the color of water, falling.

Fertility Rites For a Daughter

Enid has followed the instructions carved into
the bathroom wall at the desert service station,

hints about how to trap a child's spirit into flesh
no matter how shiny and quick, no matter
how much like a ribbon escaping out a car window

she has taken lessons from the crows and robins
making their nests, sticking bottle caps and barrettes
under her mattress, weaving twigs into the cracks in
her headboard

she has opened the cupboard door and taken out the salt
strewn it into stars on the floor
so a daughter will sit and stay, fascinated
by the constellations stuck to her soles

she turns off the TV Sunday nights,
humming into a different man's
neck each time, singing, *come to me, come to me,*
in a language only possibility knows

How To Make a Person (Tail and Background Optional)

it helps to draw a dotted line
down the middle of everything
you have to remember
every head is an egg

every body is just eight eggs
or maybe 7
in the case of a child
4 or 3

the eyes are two half moons
floating midway up the face
and for the nose you can use
a sideways 'S' below the eyes

the face should be located on the top egg
although you might prefer, for example,
to have a mouth that goes directly to your stomach
or eyes you can hide under your shirt
so that no one can see you watching

part way down the body on the 4th egg
you might want to put a dot for the belly button
that is the place we all start
but for drawings it is best to leave it for step 2 or 3

you can add the genitals if you wish
which are signified by short vertical
lines but they are generally covered up
by clothes so matter not at all

some may want a woman in which case
the breasts are two empty bowls a distance
of two finger spans above the belly button

as stated above the background is optional
but it is important to keep in mind there
is no person without a place and your person
may despair without the sound of a distant
train or perhaps some starling on a telephone wire

some artists recommend adding the hair
last but I prefer to add windows
as a finishing touch, as everyone
eventually needs a way to see in or out

Frankenstein's Bride

he is in me
they are in me
hands   machines

copper wires thread up my uterus

                they peel back the dermis
      peel back the fascia   the muscle
staple the layers under my breasts

my grandfather's tractor drags rotating disks
                plows my liver   my bladder

                they shoot rays into me
                they picture my bones   irradiate my blood
    my self on the screens above
    white hieroglyphs on blue paper
                            I shudder in pixels

I am shorn   the razors are my warm metal friends
my legs
my cunt   my upper lip

                they raise my ovaries with chopsticks
                white as sleeping faces   they carve smiles into
                slick pale viscera

                two thousand dead fireflies electrified
they blow on my womb   foul rat breath   try to start a fire
                they have lost something here
they will find him   the intern has disappeared
sculptors of blood and bile and circuitry   they will carve him out
of me

they ask my husband to come in
                and hold me down

Conception

an aspen and poplar sang
the rustling of leaves, the accompanying insects
small deer, white-tailed, sailed from tree to tree
the frogs and insects hummed together

she sang the feeblest notes
her crops vivid, soft and green
amid the rustling of leaves, the accompanying drip
to the soft distant music, how vividly
to his surprise, soft insects

Your Birth

Joy, of course, and a mess on the floor.
Strangers spinning round the bedside,
chlorine pools diminishing.
The light stands still in bowls outside.

You rise from the porch of your
father's undoing while the clouds
dissipate. Party goers pass
on either side, shake their shoulders
as if to boogie or make trouble.

You will do both, handful of foot and gum,
precious bowl.

Begin At the Mouth

not at the feet
those pretty pale turtles

or the belly
opalescent and soft
        as a banana slug

not the hands
quick worker ants

or the hair
baring its throat
      to the scissors each spring
shining like a doe

but the mouth,
mobile, scarred, full of sharp
              clicking

a crab with long red tongs
who pulls from my esophagus
dark bees stinging marks in the air
          these words

Definition Of a Tree

when climbed, gives a view
of other trees, houses, the street
next door, and the next

is not pleasant to lick but
feels good on your palms

leaves light green near the stem
yellow near the edges
like glass held to light
shaped like spear heads
not good to eat

branches the size of your waist
precarious for balancing
beetles crawl up your shorts

leaf cluster at the end of
branches make good
whips for a younger brother

bark gets in your hair, knots it
when you shimmy up the trunk

canopy sways at the top
rocks back and forth like a rowboat
mothers scream when they see you
up high

In it you might be Tarzan

The Weight Of the World

Claire's mother would be the queen of Claire's body
instructing each organ to hum
in harmony with her baroque melody

the doctors tell her Claire is underweight
a word Claire confuses with underwear and blushes
Claire sees the smile her mother hides behind her soft hand,
proud of her soldiers: the chocolate laxative,
the prune juice, bananas, the enema bulb like a clown's nose,
the suppositories that glisten like worms

after lunch her mother takes
Claire's hand and leads her to the toilet
then stands by the door
she says try for me, Claire, try

her mother keeps a scale under Claire's bed
weighs Claire each night
the jolt and click of it
when Claire jumps on thrills her
the way the numbers shift and flow like a river
at four Claire is 30 pounds
and her teddy bear is 3

but in the morning before her mother gets up
Claire has the lucky charms and milk to herself
she plucks out the soggy hearts
and moons from the bowl
lines them up on a paper napkin for later

the end is her favorite part
the milk translucent at the edges
reminds her of white feathers
pastel, sweet

continued…

with arms like putty-colored pipe cleaners
Claire tips the bowl to her chin and
drinks it all down

Territory

summers around our backyard pool I sat half in
her shadow the chlorine drying off me in little shivers
and held her feet while she lay dark-glassed and silent
in the striped beach chair

her ruby toenails were the throats of hummingbirds
her freckles — constellations foretelling my future
but the ragged patch
on her right foot where the tan

seemed erased drew my little girl kisses
because that part that most naked pale skin
was on my own foot in the same frog-shape

and it was by that mark I knew
        she was my mother

The Grass Eater

                        chewing what she pulled from

the lawn   insects *shickandshickandshick,* pause
in the sticky weeds   she licked the end of her braid

the milking shed made her faint   smelling bleach and
cheese and vomit from the wet concrete   the suck

suck suck of the machines   metal, rubber fingers
on the cows' tits   *don't worry, they can't feel it*

heavy breath, grunt of the animals   her older cousins
pinched her neck   she cried *stop* and rubbed the bruise

drifted through the fallow field to the faucets at the
screened-in porch, knelt and put her mouth

on the iron bitter spigot with its hot water

welts rose on her calves, thighs
from some tiny thing, biting and persistent

The Painted Wooden Leg

outside White Plains   in a horse corral with a ten-foot-high
chain link fence   a retired insurance salesman

raises tigers   he lets Claire rub her face in the eggy fur
of the cubs' bellies   feed them milk and soaked

toast from her thumb   the girl holds a cub outside
the tigers' cage   the mother's paw (big as a catcher's

mitt) can only reach so far   the cub   its mother
chirp like broken machines   at 2am   when her father's

fighting dream claws   Claire scales the fence
balances on top   her small slipping sneakers squeak

the tigers circle underneath   yawn   stretch
collapse in heaps   scratch their spines against

the meaty straw   their white bellies call   inviting

Getting It Down

Claire spends two hours at the dinner table

chewing, chewing
> *it won't go down*

        a beige paste
she can't swallow   she can
      feel tendons   strings   rubber cement
      inside it

when her mother looks at her own empty plate
and sighs

      Claire takes thumb and forefinger
pulls out the mass   soft as flesh   pink and brown
      it might have tentacles
      the texture like cardboard and sand paper

her mother won't
      leave her chair   till Claire's through

her mother doesn't understand
    I can't

    her mother's own meatloaf   limp asparagus
    limpid pool of butter   finished
    as fast as her mother could shovel
    her eyes on Claire   bright   foreign
    like some strange plant

Claire hears her friends outside
Lisa and Gordie discussing the complex rules of four square
      then the red ball bounces   with that hollow

      appetizing *ping*

The Snow Queen

insects hide underground, slow, feeble   bees fall over and twitch
her mother holds her on her lap, red tights: left foot, right   zips
her pink corduroy pants   she runs behind; swish-swish-swish
sidewalks gritty with salt

blue mittens between her teeth, her skates double blades, shoved to
the middle —sometimes she's fast   her mother smokes on a plaid
blanket   over her white knit cap the late crows
                fight in the pines

Memoir Of an Unrepentant Thief

if you were to shake my tiny sticky hand
you'd see a thin girl
with a rainbow-striped dress she's outgrown
yellowish hair matted to one side of her head

since my mother is busy reading her romances
I roam the streets and backyards with my own bare feet
when I find an unlocked neighbor's house
I head straight to their kitchen
I love the smell of other people's houses
they are so large and shiny and their
refrigerators are always full of things
good to eat like butter and milk
I love to scoop the butter from a stick
with my thumb and lick it off
sometimes also they have apples and cats
which are fun in their own way
(if they let me touch them)
I go into the living room and sit cross legged
in front of the TV and watch Sesame Street
until someone comes home to find me

The Closet

her mother's winter
jacket drapes her face
stink of violets and fertilizer

she bangs her naked toes against metal points
her father's golfing shoes

she wants to cry but can't
they'll hear

sticks her thumb
then three fingers in her mouth

outside the leopard circles,
coughing and panting
the claws of wild peacocks
scrabble on the roof

In Stitches

the hum *click* slower and faster
of the sewing machine, the needle a big fish
        feeding from the bottom
of my mother's hand, the tiny light
a glass eye hovering over her
                            fingers

she unfolds the transparent
human-colored paper, slides off my shirt
so she can wrap the pattern around me
        mark space with a pencil

I hold my breath
the hair on my arms
                rising

The Family Practice

Claire was turning thirteen the way milk turns,
becomes thicker, more complicated, fragrant.

She saw the man with his arthritic fist
and drill in her mouth as a trembling prophet
because he had suffered; been in a war,
lost a daughter to a drunk in a car.
Claire knew pain brought wisdom.

As his pick slipped off her gums
he whispered about the language
used in the dark churches, the old country
a code no Queens girl could break.

He was a man, he knew things
and her mother trusted him.

When he said, *this time, I think
we don't need Novocain,*
Claire didn't want to disappoint. She said yes —
a word everyone wanted from her — she understood that,
and when the drill came, with its scent of burning feathers,
its high thunder in her head,
she knew what was expected.

When it was done, he saw she was quiet,
saw she made no protest. He told her she was
good, *patient like a saint,* he said.

Tristessa

we gave each other horse names
and galloped around the edges
of the soccer field during recess
I held strands of your long soft pelt
behind you as if they were reins
we clucked to each other when
we wanted to move, the clicking
of the tongue riders use along with
their heels, a sound like stuttering
cicadas, when the boys hit you and
made you fall down I hit them back

you were twelve and you used pills,
not very many, the first time you tried
to unravel

My Friend Flicka

two girls: frequently upside down and restless
dusty bare feet on armrests
give their mothers the evil eye

braid each other's long greasy blond hair
draw horses on their notebooks   horses on
their mirrors   their magic markers smell like
bubble gum

no one watches as they stand in the
pool   they roast in their bikinis
talk slowly then fall asleep
later forget what was said

behind their mothers' backs they fight
and bite each other   deny it all later
their necks smell like hay and rotten apples
they refuse to shower or use soap   chlorine
turns their hair spring green

when their parents aren't home they take
vodka & rum from the hidden cupboard
sip it in juice glasses and make faces

they are drunk they get headaches
    and kiss each other
     to practice for boys

Truth Or Dare

I was 12, my fifth sleepover,
but this one was serious —
outdoors, no parents, a bonfire.

Wearing a flannel nightgown gone too tight
around the shoulders since May, the ribbons
frayed into bits of cloud around my neck.
Barefoot in the grass and cool dirt,
we darted like minnows.

So fun it was almost something you could eat.

Around midnight it came down
to it, our lips bruised by grape soda,
our stomachs festooned with Doritos and anxiety:
the game. I took Dare
because Truth was my father and too scary.

I let those girls (some I didn't know,
one who breathed me to sleep
every night on the phone) lead me
to the rabbit hutch. I crawled
in head first, the entrance a small tunnel,
as if I were being birthed in reverse.

Inside I squatted, my head near
my muddy bare feet, so I could fit.
A girl held the door
and when I nodded, shut it.

Are you sure, are you really sure?
she said, and I nodded, and she slipped
the latch down.
I reached my fingers through the chicken wire,
gripped as if it were a rope
saving my life. I saw the sugar-stoned girls
with their small glad hands
would tender my release. For once,
I felt safe.

Muscular Wrist

condensation
        on our small windows

sudden   sugared   syrup

these breasts weird as witches
reek of singing insects

        nipples sting like bedbugs
        like the dark eyes of drowned does

silver skin, feathered with the hair
                of pale cows,
    coated with sweat
        like weasel piss and milk

            your toes architectural
little firm boxes, all in a row,
    each a perfect snail shell

each
    the size
    of a coin
in my mouth

I could die from you

Susan

in the homeless shelter where we worked
everyone always confused our names
we were both white blonde
both a little distant with a milky film
over our blue eyes

every day we took each other to lunch
and you ate from both plates
cursing me for ordering so much rich meat
while I looked out the window and wrote
poems in my head

you were the first one to offer your breast
to that machine that ground and squeezed
after they took out the lump
you wanted me to see the hole

in the bathroom
I didn't want to look but you
pulled down your blouse anyway
so I stared at your mouth, greenish
our angry bruise

Leap

thumb-smudged face descending in the water her eyes are closed dark hair unfurls to the surface bone buttons close her calico dress dots of white flowers on navy her eyes are closed she sees redwing blackbirds shifting in branches stabs of red the female a brown spot against black sunlight sifting strong through the maple leaves her eyes are closed her skin bluer bluer she slips deeper into the river her petticoats ripple tiny bubbles like slow rising pearls the current pulls her forward down her eyes are closed her palms open as she spins slowly the laces to her black boots flare out last summer she spun in the wheat first slowly then faster faster palms up to catch the sun arms wide like a tree flung up against the horizon she remembers falling too dizzy to catch herself her eyes closed

Ecstasy At 3PM

this time
        Claire's made sure
                to lock the door

when she does it
        under the sheets
        her legs feel as if they
                lifted themselves away

        trembling, reddened
        she shudders

smells the spoiled eggs of the starlings again
        hears their *crack! whirl!*
                behind her headboard

the Virgin manifests
        in the water stain
                on the ceiling   her eyes downcast
                                          modest
                            pale finger to her lips

Claire knows she's always watching

        irises multiply
                between her legs
    the stamens scratch her thighs

she hides a razor blade
        under her tongue
                pulls it out
                          to help them along

Claire On Sunday

she wakes up
        in the hospital (still in restraints)

padded cuffs around her wrists
                her feet drumming a tattoo
spit matting her hair to her cheek

        overhead
the light fixture from her bedroom when she was
   ten, full of black flies

it speaks to her   crystal edges humming

     it sees her mother is about to come in
Claire can't see the door   the light won't let her
         turn her head   but she knows   her mother's

standing there on the cusp her mother's mental implements
      in her doctor's coat

  and the light coaxes Claire out of the covers
           until she's floating two feet up

            swimming in chords of violent gardenia perfume
      tasting the breasts of her aunts, the lawns of her neighbors,
    the skies full of planes

    Claire's in heaven   black and cold   no oxygen and the stars
bite her shoulders   they talk in low, neutral voices
                        about dates
                                and times and dosages

                                                God comes
to speak to Claire   pulling light bulbs from his mouth
              but she can't hear because of the angels singing

like loud rain underwater   they pull her down and down, hands
              on her wrists and ankles
                                    she's worried she'll never see
God again and that
I'll never get to tell him what I know

Starling

Wings gleaming
like the slick oiled
lids of a woman's eyes
in an empty bar.
Everyone and
no one at once.

If you stand still
enough in the sun
it will come,
vain brother to the
crow, blue simmer
of feathers,
landing oh so delicately
to grasp at your
spread thumb
and peck
whatever you
offer from your palm.

The Holy Birds Of Queens

across from the dry cleaners
with the duct-taped window pane

the starlings surround Claire
as she steps off the curb

shimmer and hiss and *woot*
voices like gears constantly winding
like the rising sound at the end of a question

birds so dark in the depths
of the street's one pine
the shadows enclose them like envelopes

purple bits of glint for eyes and the sound
of fluttering (they shove and adjust)
the exclamation of a yellow beak

    whistle whistle crackle

they tug at her pink purse   alight
on her shoulders   take her earlobe
in their beaks like a piece of nectarine

on her way to her day program
the starlings stain Claire's dress
    with white streaks
like she's half-erased

Activities Of Daily Living

The poster over his desk says *Hang In There, Baby,* above a kitten dangling from a branch. The kitten opens its mouth and blinks at Claire. She looks away. On the other wall a Picasso rearranges itself. Woman on the beach. As Claire watches, the pieces of the woman begin to drift away — one fades into the horizon, another sinks into the sand. Claire picks at her fingernail polish. The doctor continues to write something in her chart. A trio of purple irises leer at her from the plastic vase on his desk. One leans over his elbow and watches him write, then stares up into his face. *Obnoxious,* Claire thinks. *So,* the doctor says, finally turning to Claire. He straightens the seams in his slacks. *How are the voices?*

Joy School

for Joseph Cornell

Why is it that when people speak
of joy or paint
its substance, the canvas is a vast
blue sky or an acre of snow, broken
maybe by a few black boughs.

My joy teaches me small:
tiny and dark with delicate moving parts
in the shadows,
like the ripple of a salmon gill
under the river
or a small vintage machine
with obscure purpose and many
gears whirring.

My joy is not made in the huge
bright handclap of God.
It is made by tiny mice paws
in the mud. It is made of straw
and teeth,
with a few white feathers.

Perpetual Baptism

The smell is hard to define, gets into Claire's eyes. Her mother sits in the bleachers, buttoning and unbuttoning her pink cardigan. Three times a week they're here; exercise is supposed to help with the side effects. Claire clings to the side of the pool and adjusts her navy blue one-piece. It sags at her ass. Since she turned 30 and decided to stop eating meat (it sinks into her bones, keeps her clinging to the earth like lead diving weights), her dresses have enlarged two sizes. Her period stopped.

Two dark children splash and yell at the other end of the pool, their voices echoing off the concrete ceiling. Everything is painted peach. Claire watches the crack in the ceiling get bigger. Her mother claps her hands, mouths *Get Started,* and Claire ducks her head underwater, swims along the bottom for a few yards. A milky film stirs up, reaches for her. The medication makes it so hard to move. She'll just sit for a moment and rest. She looks up through the water and sees the ceiling crack open. The navy blue sky is filled with huge stars. One of them has His face.

The Saint Of Difficult Furniture

my sister understood your language
she paid her toll   ripped out her
eyes rather than   see the devil

cut out her tongue   when she knew
she was going to speak ill of our father

I still stumble   bruise my palms
when I cross her bridge   a handful of red hair
caught in the broken guardrail

I start out small   just a tiny letting
from the ankles with a dull knife

it's how we show we're true
pure as the hum of a fresh bucket of milk

your words will fling
themselves from my tongue

like footprints   dark   wet
climbing a golden ladder
out of this   dirt back yard

Modern Maid

Joan of Arc works at the Gap.
Her armor, nearly invisible under
the florescent light, catches on the sweaters
she folds; cashmere threads
follow her everywhere, a crimson cape.

She can't remember how she got here:
most days, can't remember her name,
but knows where her keys are,
and what bus to take to work.

God speaks to her sideways,
flickering reflections in the
napkin dispenser at the diner,
upside down when she licks
the ice cream clean from her spoon.

Joan sees pinions behind her when she uses the ATM.
There's angels, sometimes angry and frightening,
often white, and always in her dreams.
They smell like straw and milk...

Joan is sixteen. She's always sixteen.
She has freckles and is serious,
chews off her lipstick.
She'll heal you if you ask nice,
and go back behind the 501s with her.
Her name means "God is gracious."
Sometimes when she's stacking the perfume
called *heaven*
she remembers this is true.

The Cul-De-Sac Angel

with wings made of safety pins,
used tampons and bottlecaps,
softly swoops down and kisses the place under
the left breast
of all the middle-aged single women
in Ohio
whose bras are too tight, who
get a little sore spot right there,
on the fragile skin
over the heart —
every night before each
of those women
takes her last breath
before dreaming
of kisses she'll never have,
or had but never wanted,
she feels a tingle
right there —
like the start of a heart attack
or the glowing thumbprint of a saint
or how a thumbprint might feel
if a saint were to touch her
or anyone
to touch her:
Anyone who wasn't
coolly shaking
her hand
        goodbye

Aspirin

in my dream you're dead
we're talking on the phone

the old fashioned kind with
a cord that embeds itself in
fingers then twirls and twirls
on its own fascinating cats
who jump on anything that moves
with a bit of strangeness

and you're talking about my
father how you've met him now

you say he's lost weight or so
he tells you

and I keep trying to change
the subject: do you wear shoes,
did your headache stop and is
there light everywhere

hung in the trees like apples
shooting from your fingertips
like spider webs

is there light and is there
soft cake in heaven?

March 25, 1911

"One girl held back after all the rest and clung
to the window casing until the flames from the
window below crept up to her and set her clothing
on fire. Then she jumped far over the net..."
— eyewitness report, Triangle Shirtwaist Fire

she had worn swallow wings
pinned to her hair,
a whole dark sparrow poised
and fixed on the crown of her hat

she had paid a months wages
for the silk blouse the exact
color of bluebirds hanging
above her broken mattress

when she slept through the chattering
of her three roommates, she ran
and ran and ran in the fields
of her father's farm, waving her arms,
but she never got more then ten feet
off the ground, sometimes her bare feet
brushing the tops of the apple trees

now is her chance
poised at the open window
her long skirt smoking at the hem

the fire moaning and tearing behind her
the screams have almost stopped

the firemen with their tiny hoses
15 feet below on too-short ladders

continued...

some girls hold hands
as they step out
into the air

but this one, as in a dream,
closes her eyes and
takes to the sky alone

Cannibals

Qualities Of Sugar

it is white and sometimes it is brown

on the kitchen floor it attracts ants

sometimes in the bag during the summer
if it's kept low down on the bottom shelf
you will encounter little black maggots,
already dead, when you open the flap

when you try to wipe it off on your shorts
it clings to your hands and folds into rolls of dirty
white grit in the creases of your palms

it doesn't feel very good if you just put
a tablespoon on your tongue
it can choke you, going down
and then you need some pepsi

your dentist gives you lollipops, which have sugar

when you try to lift the whole bag
by yourself and it rips and spills
into a tiny beach just for dolls
then your mother will be disappointed
it can make her sigh

you often add it on top of bread or cheese
to see if they will taste better

when it is frozen in the form of a green popsicle
you and your brother will hit each other
in the face to get it first

continued…

when you mix it with water in a clear glass
it moves about a bit
and disappears

sometimes at night it's all that's left and it's enough
to keep you busy a short while until you realize
the house is empty
and you begin to howl

Children Having Trouble With Meat

    they're not sure?

        the fork   makes an
interesting clang when they bang it
      on the rim of the plate

      in the center
          there's something?

it makes no noise when they hit
        it with their fork
               not even a grunt

      although when they hold their ear
                very close
to its burning smell

          there is a wet
            hiss

The Cannibals

Someone is bleeding, we see the spots
on the carpet, check yourself, *check*

yourself for cuts, we murmur, mill
about, slowly raising our palms,

inspecting our elbows and buttocks,
the French maid enters the great

hall and we tell her of our concern,
someone is bleeding, we say, *look*

the spots are fresh, she is silent,
unamused, removes the stale

croissants with a flourish, *check
yourself,* someone calls after her,

then great chocolate labs stream
through the French doors, we try

to grab their collars as they dash past,
their paws, their eyes need inspecting,

they could be bleeding, it happens all
the time to dogs you know, large insensate

beasts, but they elude us, rapid and soft
as a brown river of sparrows, the hall

fills with thumping echoes for a moment
after they pass, *someone is bleeding,*

someone says, but it is time for lunch
and we all return to what we were doing

before someone was bleeding: chess,
model boats, detailed sketches

of imaginary cathedrals.

A Tender Age

in this corner, a dog is screaming

he is calling your name
Oliver, Oliver

you have better things to do

you in your urchin shirt
rusty shoes, hat full
of night and spiders

you sneak the hubcaps
off dead men's eyes

you borrow morning
ransom it for some
chilled red soup

you tuck bracelets, brooches,
feathered hat pins in your pockets

they clank an odd song when you run
they rub together like bones in your thin
shoulder joints

no meat   no meat

for the strangers' mouths

for the dog still barking

for the profiles made of metal and gems

when the street lights pop on
so many bad ideas over so many
dusty, perfumed heads

you are just getting started
your business hawking pocket watches
stealing time and other boys'
tender teeth

Supplies

rancid meat
dark meat
broken meat
black meat
meat with the teeth
        still in it
yellow meat
meat under the half-moon
meat in the bathtub
meat wrapped in shower curtains
                          & duct tape,
sunk with rocks in the Jersey swamp

The Transparent Dinner

At eight, my mother brings the turkey pot pie
to our table. I gage the gleam in her eye.

She paces around the edges, touching each
of us on the shoulder. She refuses to sit down,

slips off to feed the animals. My father pours
glasses of milk from the pink pitcher, passes

them to me and my brother. My brother and I
look at each other from across the table. He is

smaller than me; his chin barely reaches the
tabletop. He looks up. We can hear Mother's

footsteps in the room above us. She appears
to be dragging something. Anxiety wrinkles

waves into my brother's forehead. The plates
are huge, blue and white, covered with

oriental men carrying fish and women down
a mountain in baskets, castles built of

curlicues and children waving as if to warn
from the balconies. My father cuts into the pie.

The knife releases steam — it smells like love,
like fresh bread and garlic and cloves

and something else. My father passes slices
to my brother, to me. My brother watches me.

I will do it first. I lift up my fork and begin to eat.

How the Witch Got Started

for Hansel and Gretel

the snow outside
      had blocked the doors
they had already burnt   the curtains for fuel
the light outside was pitiless

chandelier crystals hung
      from pink threads
   at the window

the only things left in the cupboard were
              salt and baking soda

I love you so I'll eat you up,
      someone said to the mother when she was
          little

the mother still remembers her first sight of her daughter
she came out of my body
      yanked out with a gasp that felt like
 a fist in the belly
         gleaming, red as a candied apple,
        bloody as a   steak

she cried
      with the children when they had to eat
the kittens   the soup lasted a week

Annabeth tried to hide some bones in a shoebox
in the coat closet, ring of dried violets, black scarf

we can have the memorial later, the mother told her,
right now we have to eat

the days were shorter and shorter
        they had eaten the candles
some of the children had diarrhea for days

she would save her daughter's hair,
                      she told herself
she would keep it in a locket for next time

in the end there was
 very little difference
      between sleeping
          and waking

the children were too
        tired to move   they wet the bed

she began to pray   they would
                not wake up

even though they didn't speak
            their eyes   blank suffering   made
                    her leave the room

afterwards
                the mother found a spot next to
                    Wendy's bed where
                    Wendy had started to
                        eat the wall

     the mother did not ask the children to do this
only *she* ate them   afterwards she knew
                her daughter was safe
              she would never
                  be alone

                          continued…

        she wanted to
remember their names
      carved them into the
            frame around her
   mirror

how could anyone say she hadn't done
                     her best?

if she were gone   who would take care
                  of her babies?

in the spring
    she was left
        with only two

they ran from her
    and disappeared into the forest
as soon as the snow melted

she never   saw them again
    she misses those ones the most

        she knew they would
              tell tales

Gretel Dreams With Her Eyes Open

vertebra, bowl, moon
        collarbones, shin bones

wobbling, shimmering, shining
        glowing, shifting

                      every day the bones
            grow closer   to the surface

she eats water and dirt   her belly
        stretches tight as an eggplant
                her ribs musical bars

everything is gaining clarity
        her cheekbones   her chin
                so close to the moonlight now

        clavicle, humerus   she hoarded
mud pies under her bed

        iliac crest
                she's too tired to walk
                      much further

What We Think About the Missing Girl

if her hair had a voice it would sing
low and wordless yet musical

when no one appears to be listening
we refer to her hair
using words like "pelt" and "feral" and "river"

sometimes when we are talking about the governments
of foreign lands and rebels and the need for change,
supplies and fresh fruit we are actually talking about her hair

and sometimes when we dream about a sweet pale liquid
and wake up in the dark, our lips cracked,
our eyes wet, we are dreaming about her hair

when our president on TV moves his right hand
forcefully and talks in bold, sweeping generalizations,
he is thinking about her hair

before our old men die, when they are staring upwards
and the room dims, their last vision is of her hair
falling slowly towards them, a gold curtain

My Favorite Sacrifice

slow music, star tattoos at your wrists: we toss you towards the sky, catch you as your hair flares out, a dark exclamation, blue eye shadow under an empty tree, you draw on your breasts with magic marker, your hair like broken glass embedded in a knee, you fall in love with a crow, your eyes change color, a wolf, something swimming fast underwater, your neck long, ethereal, yellow; seems made for knives or hands,
sometimes there's a dark cloth over your eyes,
sometimes in your mouth
sometimes you say *yes*, sometimes you refuse

late in the day, a cliff, a fire, some water

You and Your Animal Teeth

You think I am so
fascinated by what
you are saying, but
I am just watching
your animal teeth,
the ragged, raw row,
stained and cracked,
your lips a reddish loveseat
not quite covering
the cannibal skeleton underneath.

What Hansel In His Cage Is Forgetting

                    how his hair loosened at night
in his old bed and how the mice
carried it away

the morning his stepmother
boiled pine needles and dirt
        served it
                to him and his sister
                      with salt

        how it hurt to lie down
his bones so close to the skin
shivering in the dark

the deep red
        circles under his father
             the woodcutter's eyes,
how his father let his beard grow
        until little worms moved in

how a small stone feels when
              he sucks it

how the white pebbles banged
bruises into his thighs, so heavy
                in his pockets

how, when she unwrapped the crust from her pinafore,
Gretel's wrists were so sharp
                looking hurt his eyes

continued...

how, when he took Gretel's hand
                in the forest
                          as the white bird led them
to the house made of food,
        he knew they were
             saved

In the Witch's House, Gretel Remembers

    the sheen of the white pebbles
            in the moonlight lit up like
                  blinking eyes

how she once killed a mouse
        with a hammer
            made soup
just for her and her brother

    how she chipped her tooth
eating the stewed sole of her father's boot
        how Hansel gave her half of his

how the skin on her shoulders
        was so transparent
the straps
        of her underclothes wore holes,
        the sores gleamed like pennies

how her breath mingled with
Hansel's the second night out in the woods,
        when he told her the story

about a large white bird
            that would ferry them home
                across the river,
            their pockets full
        of cookies and pearls

The Next Season

       the witch has started over now
has begun to forget her old name

       has hundreds of jars of pickled fruit
and meat in her coat closet

       she carries a loaf of bread
everywhere in her purse

she offers sweets
       to other parents' children

       she is large now   she has splintered a chair
just by sitting

       the doctor recommends
vegetables   steamed   only once a day
       he asks her about her diet
              and she says nothing

RRH

girl   wolf   thin white fingers entwined in stinking fur
flashes of color (he's colorblind   he can't make
it out) a large fluttering surface   whipping in the wind
(or the wind she makes by running)   whipping like a tail
(a tail) like a shadowy flag   a coat of arms   a bundle of bones
a collection of grandmamma moans   fur sprouts faceward
her teeth root down deeper   his teeth root down deeper
white gleams underneath the hood   tied under the chin (sharp
as a knife   white as a tooth)   tied to a tree
the fleas don't bother her   the pink welts small and sexy
tiny nipples all over her throat   her basket spills down the path
he lays down before her   belly up   waiting for a scratch

The Wedding Night

His hand on the back of a fox,
my husband shuffles in, kicks
the door shut behind him with
his heel, and says. Staring at my

neck with the eyes of Mary after
she found the lamb. As he fingers
his long braid, smelling of jasmine

and bone dust. My husband says.
My husband with the crooked
crown, with the half-seeing eye.

With the thumb that wanders
while he sleeps. My husband limps
to the fireplace, trailed by the be-

spectacled dog and bear; my husband
lifts the lid. To the murmuring,
bubbling, black-bellied pot. The pot

says, *get your filthy feet off my new
red carpet*, before my husband.
Tipping the bitter soup into the fire.

The fire dying, cursing, spitting. He says,
Don't. My husband says, *Don't let your
fairytales get in the way of my mouth.*

About the Author

Christine Hamm is a PhD candidate in English Literature at Drew University, where she was awarded a Caspersen Scholarship for Academic Promise. In 2007, she was a runner up to Queens' Poet Laureate. Her poetry has been published in *The Adirondack Review, Pebble Lake Review, Horseless Press, Lodestar Quarterly, Women's Studies Quarterly, Blue Fifth Review, Poetry Midwest, MiPoesias, Rattle, Snow Monkey* and *Exquisite Corpse*, among others. She has been nominated twice for a Pushcart Prize, and once for "The Best of the Web". Her work has been anthologized in *Homewrecker: An Adultery Reader* and *The Murdering of Our Years: Artists and Activists on Making Ends Meet*, both by Soft Skull Press. Her full-length book of poems, *The Transparent Dinner*, was published by Mayapple Press in October '06. Christine on the editorial board of several literary journals, including *Ping Pong*. She teaches English at York College and has taught poetry writing in NYC and New Jersey. She has edited many poetry anthologies, including *We Taste Like Presents* and *A Strange Kind of Food*. She has three chapbooks, *Children Having Trouble with Meat*, published by MiPoesias, *The Animal Husband*, published by Dancing Girl Press, and *The Salt Daughter* by Little Poem Press. *Dampen*, her latest chapbook, is due out from Pudding House. She has been featured on local and national radio and television, and has performed all over the country. For more about her, go to chamm.blogspot.com.

Photo by Mathew David Powell

www.ingramcontent.com/pod-product-compliance
Lightning Source LLC
Chambersburg PA
CBHW052114070526
44584CB00017B/2475